This book is dedicated to those who wrestle every scrum, compete for every lineout and never miss a tackle — from the safety of their sofa.

First published in 2011 by Hurricane Press Ltd
PO Box 568, Cambridge, New Zealand
www.hurricane–press.co.nz

Copyright © 2011 Hurricane Press Ltd

Illustrations: Ross Payne

National Library of New Zealand Cataloguing-in-
Publication Data

Sharp, Jack, 1954-
You're a real rugby fan when-- / by Jack Sharp.
ISBN 978-0-9864522-9-1
1. Rugby football—New Zealand—Humor.
2. New Zealand wit and humor. 3. New Zealand—
Social life and customs—Humor.
I. Title.
NZ828.302—dc 22

Printed by Bookbuilders, China.

Hurricane Press
books that blow you away

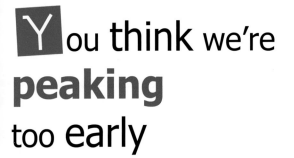

You think we're **peaking** too early

Your Most Valuable Player is your **designated driver**

You've shaved the **number 11** into your eyebrows

The TV commentators mimic **everything** you say

Going for a **quick bite** normally refers to someone's ear

Your *proudest* moment **was** *starting a* **Mexican wave** *that did **four*** circuits

You swap your son's **rugby figurines** for Monopoly money

You wonder whether **Mr and Mrs Meads would** have done an **undies ad**

It's easier to complete a PHD than figure out the new rules

You wouldn't mind **seeing** a few **farmers** in the side

Having a **crack** around the **fringes** isn't as **dodgy** as it sounds

You **don't know** whether to feel **sorry** for **the mascot** or **trip him up**

You **dislocate** your **collar bone** reaching for the **remote**

1t **amazes** you funerals are held the day of a test match

You can **name** the **top try scorer** since records began but can't **remember** your anniversary

You have read **185 books** in your life. All rugby **biographies**

You haven't **tackled** anyone for years but **the ref** is seriously tempting you

If your team wins
you say **we won**.
If they **lose**, you say
they lost.

Coming out **hard** is **just** what the coach is after

Watching the **losing captain** being interviewed is a **match highlight**

'Great tackle'
should be heard on
the field, **not**
in the
showers

You **hope** the
s–t–r–e–a–k–e–r
is a **chick**

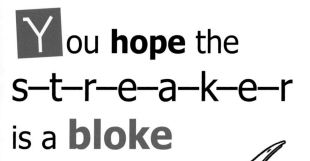

You **hope** the
s–t–r–e–a–k–e–r
is a **bloke**

You'd rather buy **another round** than fork out for the **rugby channel**

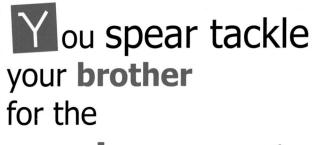

You spear tackle your **brother** for the **couch**

Every game has a **ref** with a face you just want to **punch**

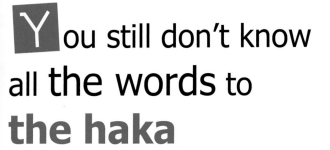

You still don't know all **the words** to **the haka**

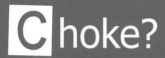 **C**hoke?

You've **gotta** be
choking?

You've built a **grandstand** in the kitchen

You **wonder** what happened to half–time **oranges**

You watch the **entire replay,** smugly knowing we won

You envy the guy in the **crowd** who packed **bacon sandwiches**

You envy the same guy who **smuggled** in four bottles of **whisky**

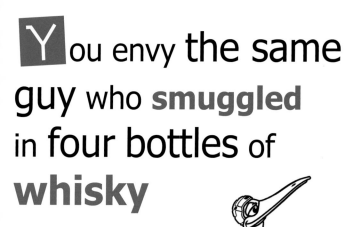

You hate
talkback callers.
But you call
talkback
when we lose

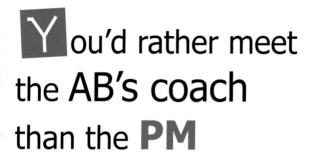

You'd rather meet
the AB's coach
than the **PM**

You take your **eight–week–old baby** into the terraces (with some formula)

You practise scrumming against **hay bales** in the paddock

You watch replays of **games** played seven years ago and still get **excited**

You've **lost count** of Jonah's **wives**

You can't fit the **car** in the **garage** because **you** bought the **posts** from Athletic Park

Despite **years** of training your **bladder** can't go the full 80

You **block** your ears the entire day so you don't **hear the score**

You name your **goldfish**
Walter **and** Buncey

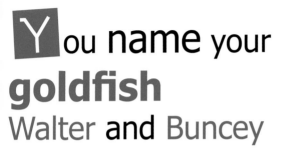

There can **never** be too many replays. There can **never** be too many replays.

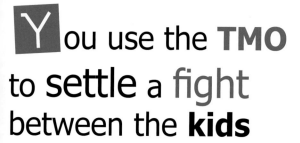

You use the **TMO** to settle a fight between the **kids**

A kids' party booked for 2.30 on a **Saturday arvo** is cause for divorce

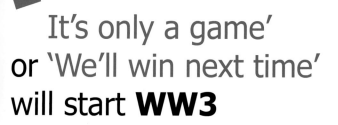

It's only a game'
or 'We'll win next time'
will start **WW3**

You remember when
match tickets
cost less than a
second hand
car

The **BLACK jersey**
will go a lot further
than NCEA

Dressing up as a **nun** or **superhero** is entirely acceptable. As long as your **mates** join you

You don't consider **Sevens** a *real* **sport** – but will take the Olympic **gold** if we **win**

you're still wearing your team's **face paint** at your Monday morning board meeting

A draw is like kissing your **sister**

Training used to involve shearing and docking, not **poncing** around a gym

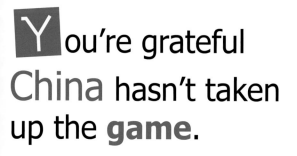

You're grateful China hasn't taken up the **game**.

Yet.

You agree cheerleaders are a **great addition** to the modern game. Unless it's your **daughter**.

You're aiming for 15 grandkids so you can have a **whole team**

Vuvuzelas might be **annoying** but they make a perfect **y**ard glass

"Four more years is still **ringing** in your **ears**

Practising the
up and under
isn't **appropriate**
in the **workplace**

You mocked **shoulder pads** in the 80s. Now you wear them on the field.

During **golden oldies** a player says you've **dropped** your **mouth guard**. It's your **false teeth**

You divide the
bathroom in two –
Home
and
Away

Yelling at the TV has **no effect** on the game, but makes you feel better **dammit**

You give the opposition's team bus directions. To the **wrong city**.

A dead rubber calls for a **big night.** A **big match** requires solitary **confinement**

The rotation system
is fine so long as
the coach
is included

You would rather
sit in the driving
rain than with
the tossers
in the corporate box

You'd rather be drinking **free booze** than getting **soaked** on the terraces

The family already knows your **epitaph**: 'He was doing it all day, ref!'

Supporting your local hooker is a **good thing**

You've never been strong at spelling but have no issues with Rococoko, **Dallaglio** and van der Westhuizen

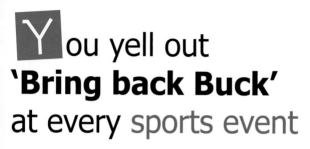

You yell out
'Bring back Buck'
at every sports event

You tell whoever's in front of the telly to either sit down or leave the room before a vital kick

You take a picture of the **scoreboard**

after **every** game

You drive to the game with **flags** on the **car aerial** and a foam f👆nger out the window

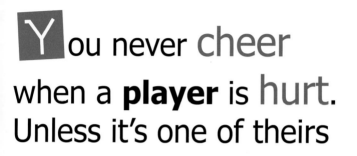

You never cheer
when a **player** is hurt.
Unless it's one of theirs

Each season you repeat, 'Oh, **God**, if we get **this kick** I'll **never** ask for anything again'

You think **drop goals** should be **outlawed** unless you **win** with one in the **last minute**

Everyone knows where they were when Diana died. You know where **you** were when **Umaga** made **THAT** spear tackle

You **defriend** anyone who tapes the game and **watches** it later

You refuse to forgive the **player** who gets drunk in public and urinates in the bar. Unless they score the **match winning try**

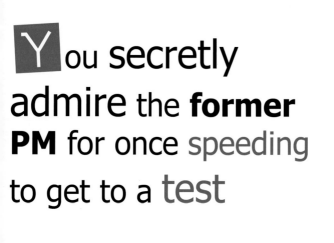

You secretly admire the **former PM** for once speeding to get to a test

You have to **sell** a **family member** to pay for **food** at the ground

You don't need to **book** into a **salon** to get a **facial**

Having a **workmate** who **supports** the **opposition** is hilarious when you win

You read the most important part of the paper first – where your team sits on the points ladder

Work/life balance is *extremely* important, providing it revolves around **home games**

You dress your **toddler** in your team's kit before they **know** any **better**

You watch
the game on TV
but listen to
radio
commentary

You love taking **American football** fans to games because their sissy heroes wear helmets and knee pads

1t's fine to wear fingerless gloves on the field providing you eat quiche and canapés after

1n the pub quiz you correctly guess the **USA** as most recent Olympic gold medallists*.

(*Paris, 1924).

You wonder whether it's really necessary for the gay rugby world cup to be bi-annual

1t's common knowledge that if the **national side** lose the dollar goes **down** and crime goes **up**

The screams from the lounge prompt a concerned neighbour to drop by, mistaking it for a family row

It's time to call it a day when half the team can't pass a kidney stone or score in a brothel

You've been told **concussion** doesn't affect sqdmWxefWey

Kicking a **pig's bladder** any other time would **prompt** calls to the SPCA

Scalping is to be **frowned** upon.

Unless **you** get them for **a steal**

HD is considered a **household expense**

You buy a **house** opposite the **stadium** so you don't have to **drive**

If you enjoyed this book, don't miss these!

You're a real Kiwi when . . .
by Justin Brown

It's a real Kiwi summer when . . .
by Jack Sharp

New Zealand 50 Australia 0
by Jack Sharp

www.hurricane-press.co.nz